THE HAIL MARY
Its Meaning and its Origin

By Fr. René Laurentin

Translated from French by
The Int'l Marian Research Institute
The Marian Library
University of Dayton, Ohio 45469

By: Bro. William Fackovec, S.M.

Edited and Published by
FAITH PUBLISHING COMPANY
P.O. Box 237
Milford, Ohio 45150

Published by Faith Publishing Company
For additional copies, write to:
>Faith Publishing Company
>Box 237
>Milford, Ohio 45150

This book originally published as "Je vous salue Marie" by Desclée De Brouwer, Paris, France, July 1990.

Copyright © 1991, Faith Publishing Company

Library of Congress Catalog Card No.: 91-071542

ISBN: 0-9625975-7-0

Scriptural Text: Confraternity of Christian Doctrine
>copyright 1970, (New American Bible).

Table of Contents

The Hail Mary

Hail Mary, Full of Grace,
The Lord is With Thee.
Blessed are Thou Amongst Women,
And Blessed is The Fruit of Thy Womb,
Jesus.

Holy Mary, Mother of God,
Pray for us sinners,
Now, and at the hour
of our death, Amen.

Introduction

An Uninterrupted Symphony

Without a doubt the **Hail Mary** is the prayer, the one formula, that is most often and most incessantly repeated throughout the world. Millions of Catholics say it and repeat it each day, from fifty to one hundred and fifty times and more, when reciting a chaplet, or rosary, whether during the day or during sleepless nights. The number is astronomical, incalculable, inestimable.

What is the reason for this unique frequency?

Some Objections

There are several reasons for surprise here.

1. From the beginning, the golden rule for Christian prayer has been that it be addressed to God through Christ. The first of prayers is the one that Christ taught us: the **Our Father.** The principal liturgical prayers: the collects, the anaphoras of the Mass are, similarly, addressed to the first person of the Holy Trinity. And yet in the rosary, where there are ten **Hail Marys** for one **Our Father** (or in the *Angelus* with its three **Hail Marys**), this prayer to Mary holds the record for frequency of repetition.

Does the heart have reasons that the mind does not know of? Or better still, does reverence for the transcen-

dence of God lead us to approach Him through that marvelous creature to whom God confided Himself, that He
might become man, and to whom He confided us before
dying (*"Behold your mother" John* 19:27)?

Mary was chosen to bring God to humanity: to teach
the Son of God how to smile and how to speak as man;
and reciprocally, she received the grace to bring mankind
to God.

Let us not forget that the **Hail Marys** of the Rosary are
structured and controlled by the **Our Father** which begins
each decade. Quantity yields to quality. Human prayer is
so lowly, so difficult, that it can rise but gradually; and
the road to the invisible God appears so steep to man
(and all the more so to the sinner), that he really needs
preliminary steps before coming to the Father, the object
of every prayer. Blessed are those who arrive at this end
and who with Mary and with Jesus Christ Himself in the
unity of the mystical body say: **Our Father.**

2. Another objection comes from Christ Himself:
Do not rattle on as the pagans do. (*Matt.* 6:7).

Here again, quantity must not make us neglect quality.
But human frailty needs to be supported by words and
gestures, so that it does not vanish into the void, or end
in distraction. From this point of view, a certain quantity
of prayers is useful to sustain one's concern for prayer
and the habit of prayer. To say, "I look for quality and
I scorn quantity" could be quite an illusion. Sometimes
a person will no longer pray for fear of praying badly.

I knew a painter so anxious, so concerned to paint well,
that he no longer dared to set himself to the task. He
was waiting for a state of grace that never came. He did
not paint for months on end. His obsession with perfection (or I know not what fear), had rendered him sterile.
Some friends had to convince him to begin again, little

by little. "Whatever happens, begin your day by painting for at least an hour, whether well or badly."

He put himself to it and inspiration returned. In a similar way we could say to people:

"Begin your day with time for prayer, whether you do it very well or badly, and in this way prayer will come."

A multiplicity of words is useful, as an organic support for prayer, of union with God—a bodily support. Man, a rational animal, prays with his spirit, but also with his body. Prayer should involve him totally: hence there are prostrations, genuflections, joined hands, hands raised up or extended, and likewise use of the vocal chords, such as the Rosary or the Jesus Prayer call for.

Why Mary?

What puts Mary at the head of our statistics regarding prayer, meshes with the humble road of salvation in Jesus Christ, who came to us through Mary.

Certainly, Jesus Christ is the "sole mediator." (*1 Tim.* 2:5). He is God and man, become human to make us divine. He is the true Mediator: not an intermediary half-way between God and man, but a solid bridge belonging to both sides, that of God and that of man, who unites them in His person.

But there is nothing of the paternalistic in God. He does nothing in us without us, or outside us. He saves us, not from on high and from the exterior, but from the interior, within us. Salvation is of divine-human cooperation at every level. In the beginning, under the Old Covenant, He called forth the faith of Abraham; and at the beginning of the New Covenant, He called forth the most marvelous and most humble of creatures to make the Son of the transcendent God first the humble Babe of the crib, united to other men, and then on Calvary, the One crucified, the

One who died for us. A mother was necessary, not only as a means and instrument for this work of astonishing love, but as God's first and most intimate partner.

For this leading role, for this role of intimacy, God preserved her from all sin. He shared everything with her in His abasement. He continues to share everything with her now that He has raised her to Heaven. There is not a particle of the body of Jesus, when He was born, that was not given to Him by Mary, His Mother. There is not a grace of Christ raised from the dead, that He does not give and share with her. In Heaven as on earth, the law of their union is: "All that is yours is mine, and all that is mine is yours." God invites us to enter into this sharing which began (and which reaches completion) with Mary, prototype of the Church.

HISTORY OF AN ACT OF PRAISE

Whence came this prayer to Mary, the formula that is repeated more often than any other in the world? How was it formed?

In the early Church, the **Hail Mary** was not recited at all. And Mary, the first of Christians, to whom this greeting had been addressed by the angel, certainly did not say it. Even today, when she prays with seers, while holding a rosary, she does not say the **Hail Mary.** At Lourdes, when Bernadette recited the rosary in her presence, the Lady of the Grotto joined in the **Glory Be,** but "did not move her lips" while the young girl from Bigorre recited the **Hail Mary.** At Medjugorje, when the Blessed Virgin prays with the seers—the high point of each apparition—she prays with them the **Our Father** and the **Glory Be,** but not the **Hail Mary** (which they will have recited before the apparition).

When Did Praying to the Saints Begin?

The **Hail Mary** took form slowly, gradually, in the course of centuries.

Let us repeat, the essential prayer of the Church is addressed to the Father through the Son. In the Latin Missal, only two prayers were addressed to Christ: the first and third on the Feast of Corpus Christi. And there was no prayer addressed to the Holy Spirit, not even on the Day of Pentecost.

For God is the support and foundation of every prayer, which neither exists nor takes steps without Him, and leads only to Him. Why then are there prayers addressed to others than the Father? What is their function and their legitimacy?

They are secondary prayers—antiphons and hymns for example. They have as their function to actualize our links with the elect in the Communion of Saints. They are not unlawful acts of worship, contesting the essential prayer of the Church. These formulas are inscribed in prayer itself, in that impulse towards God Himself, for we go to Him together, not without intercessors, and we rediscover others in God, Who is all in all.

When then did praying to the saints begin? Very early, Christians felt a profound connection with the martyrs, who had overcome terrible sufferings in fidelity to the Lord, and their bodies prolonged the sacrifice of Christ for His body, which is the Church. (*Col.* 1:24). These faithful pointed the way of salvation. The cult of martyrs began in the second century.

After the persecutions, the renegades sought the intercession of the confessors of the faith (the survivors who sometimes bore the marks of their wounds), that they might receive a penance and be rehabilitated.

Hence, they had recourse to the martyrs, who had been

reunited with Christ by giving proof to the very end of the greatest love. (*John* 15:13).

Very soon after that, in the fourth century, and perhaps a little earlier, people began to address the holy ascetics and Mary privately.

How the Hail Mary Became a Prayer

The first word of the **Hail Mary,** *chaire,* (rejoice), which begins the angel's message to Mary, appears to have been written sometime in the third century, as part of a graffito found at Nazareth, on the wall of the house very often visited by Christians as the place of the Annunciation.

And we have found in the sands of the Egyptian desert, on a papyrus that experts also date from the third century, a prayer addressed to Mary. This prayer had been known previously, but it was believed to date from the Middle Ages. Here it is:

> "We take refuge beneath the shelter of your mercy, Mother of God. Do not reject our petitions, but in our necessities, save us from danger, you who alone are chaste and blessed."
> (Papyrus no. 470 of the John Rylands Library, Manchester).

Towards the end of the fourth century, the liturgy of certain Oriental churches selected one day to commemorate Mary, before the Feast of Christmas (the way martyrs were already being commemorated). The commemoration of Mary could take place only in connection with the Incarnation. Preachers repeated the words of the angel addressed to Mary. This was in the nature of a prosopopeia: a literary and oratorical convention in which one addresses a personage from the past. But quite soon, this prosopopeia became a prayer.

The oldest homily of this kind, attributed to Gregory of Nyssa, seems to have been given at Caesarea, in Cappadocia, between 370 and 378. This is how the homilist comments on Gabriel's greeting, bringing the Christian people into association with it:

> "Let us cry out in the words of the angel:
> Rejoice, O full of grace, the Lord is with you.
> From you arose the One who is perfect in dignity and in whom resides the fullness of the Godhead.
> Rejoice, full of grace, the Lord is with you:
> With the servant is the king.
> With the Immaculate, the One who sanctifies the universe.
> With her who is beautiful, the most beautiful of the children of men, to save men made in His image."
> (Text edited by D. Montagna in *Marianum* 24 (1962), pp. 98-105.)

Another homily, likewise attributed to Gregory of Nyssa, and intended for the same celebration, takes up, in a similar manner, Elizabeth's praise of Mary: *Blessed are you among women.* (*Luke* 1:42).

> "Yes, you are blessed among women.
> For from among all virgins you have been chosen,
> For you have been judged worthy to shelter such a Savior,
> For you have received the One who fills all things. . .
> For you have become a treasure-house of the spiritual pearl."
> (Homily wrongly attributed to Chrysostom, pp. 62, 766).

Where Does the Second Part
of the Hail Mary Come From?

The second part of the **Hail Mary:** "Holy Mary, Mother of God" has a more recent history. It has its origin in the Litany of the Saints, introduced in the seventh century. There, Mary was the first to be invoked after God: "Holy Mary, pray for us."

This formula was developed in various ways, and so here and there it was added to the biblical formula of the **Hail Mary.**

The great Italian preacher, St. Bernardine of Siena (15th century), was already saying, to that blessing which ends the *Ave:*

> *Blessed are you among women. (Luke* 1:42).

We may add:

> "Holy Mary, pray for us sinners." (Sermon on the Passion, cited by H. Leclercq in the *Dictionnaire d'archéologie et de liturgie,* 10/2, 2059).

Some breviaries from the second half of the 15th century contain this brief formula. We find it in Saint Peter Canisius in the 16th century (*Catechismus major,* 1555, Book 2, Chapter 2, paragraph 2: *De Salutatione Angelica,* F. Stricher, ed. Rome, PUG, 1933, nos. 35, 37, pp. 12-13).

The last phrase: "Now and at the hour of our death," made its appearance in a Franciscan breviary of 1525. The breviary, introduced by Pius V in 1568, adopted it. This breviary prescribed the recitation of the **Our Father** and the **Hail Mary** at the beginning of each hour. That is how our **Hail Mary** became known and promulgated in its entirety in the form that we know.

But this formula of the Roman breviary took time to spread. A number of breviaries that did not have it have disappeared. Others adopted it gradually and spread it among priests, and through them, among the people. Its integration was to be fully achieved in the nineteenth century.

The epithet "poor," placed before "sinners" in the French translation, does not exist in the Latin text. It is an addition from the French translation of the nineteenth century a humble appeal for pity and compassion. This addition, which some have criticized as excessive and redundant, expresses a double truth: the poverty of the sinner and the place given to the poor in the Gospels. "Blessed are the poor," Jesus proclaims, and among these, He includes sinners, to whom the good news of the Gospel is addressed in the first place:

I have not come to call the just but sinners. (Mark 2:10).

Part I

The Biblical Half
of the "Hail Mary"

CHAPTER 1

"Hail" or "Rejoice"

The first words of the **Hail Mary** are those of the Angel greeting Mary, hence the name "Angelical Salutation" given to this prayer.

How should the first word be translated? In Greek *"chaire"* literally means rejoice.

If the Latin used the word *"Ave"* (Hail), the equivalent of our "good day," "hello," it is because *chaire* (rejoice), was the "good day" among the Greeks: a "good day" that expressed joy. It seemed obvious to translate the one "good day" by another.

But in both the biblical and theological contexts, the greeting addressed to Mary had nothing of the commonplace about it. It is of an exceptional and solemn character. We see this by contrasting the two annunciations that begin the first chapter of the Gospel of Luke:

— The announcement to Zachary, father of John the Baptist (*Luke* 1:4-27);

— and the announcement to Mary (*Luke* 1:28-38).

The announcement to Zachary, who was exercising the highest priestly function, contains nothing in the nature of a greeting. But we do find a greeting in the annoucement to Mary. And this greeting is marked by an extraordinary deference. It does not answer the prayer of an old and sterile couple, nor does it announce the birth of a

3

prophetic precursor, but bears the greatest Good News: the coming of God, the Savior.

In addressing Mary, whom he will invite to become "the Mother of the Lord," the Angel takes up the words of the greetings whereby the prophets announced to Israel the eschatological coming of the Messiah, or, of God himself. This is the way the prophet Zachariah spoke, 480 years before Christ:

> *Rejoice, daughter of Zion, shout aloud, daughter of Jerusalem; for see your king is coming to you, his cause won, his victory gained, humble and mounted on an ass, on a foal, the young of a she-ass. He shall announce the peace to the nations. He shall rule from sea to sea, from the river to the ends of the earth. (9:9-10).*

This is nothing less than the announcement of messianic joy: The one who comes is the Universal King, but he comes in the garb of a poor man—as Jesus will do on Palm Sunday.

But the prophet Zephaniah, whose words the Angel Gabriel will repeat in almost their entirety, goes much further. It is not only the heir of King David who comes; it is God Himself. God in person governed His people during the Exodus. In the midst of this people, He dwelt in the tent set up for the Ark of the Covenant, during the crossing through the desert, and then in the Temple, until the Exile, when the Ark disappeared. Zephaniah announces (3:14-17) that He will return at the end of time. He will dwell within the womb of the Daughter of Sion, a personification of Israel. The Daughter of Sion designates the people of God, not just the name of the capital city, Daughter of Jerusalem (as Zachariah had said), but by the name of the holy place which is its heart—Sion. This is a select, a choice appellation, a "nec plus ultra."

The Angel of the Annunciation (*Luke* 1:28) takes up the prophecy of Zephaniah literally, and actualizes it by applying it to Mary. She is the eschatological Daughter of Sion. The comparison is detailed as follows:

Announcement of the Prophet to Israel (*Zephaniah* 3:14-17)	Announcement by the Angel to Mary (*Luke* 1:28-33)
15 Rejoice (Hebrew *ranni*) Daughter of Sion	28 Rejoice *(chaire)* Full of grace
16b Jahweh king of Israel is in your midst	The Lord is with you.
16 Fear not, O Zion Yahweh your God is in your midst	30 Fear not, Mary 31 Behold you will conceive in your womb and you shall
17 warrior-savior	bear a son and you will give him the name:
15b the King of Israel within you	Yahweh-Savior (Jesus) 33 He shall reign.

After announcing to Mary the birth of this son, who will bear the name of Savior, the Angel reveals His transcendence:

— *"He shall be great."* God alone is great, and the Bible reserves this epithet for Him. When applying it to men, the Bible relativizes the term as when it says, for example, of John the Baptist, *"He will be great before the Lord."* (*Luke* 1:15).

— *"He will be called Son of the Most High."* He comes from on high. He is the Son of God, as the Angel will confirm later on (*Luke* 1:35). In semitic usage, "He will be called" does not relativize or minimize a title, for the name is for a being revealed and manifested. We must understand this to mean: He will be, and will be recognized, as Son of the Most High. This appellation is important. It advances the revelation of the Trinity. Mary does not become Mother of Yahweh, of the Father. This would be false and would certainly be shocking to hear. She is the Mother of the Son of God, who comes among men to reveal Himself as such.

It is then an awe-inspiring, a divine greeting that is addressed to Mary, an echo of Zephaniah, as presented by the Angel Gabriel.

She will give birth to Him, who is, from all eternity, Son of the Most High, and this will be a true birth. The Angel emphasizes that she will conceive in her womb and bring forth. And this joining of transcendence and humility will continue throughout the Gospel, where Jesus will be called Lord, Savior, Salvation, Redemption of Israel, etc., but also baby *(brephis),* little child, infant.

It is only after having presented Jesus as Son of the Most High, as transcendent Savior, that the Angel calls him Messiah, heir of David, by taking up the announcement of the Prophet Nathan (*2 Sam.* 7:12-16) made to the founder of the dynasty. Much of that passage is repeated by the Angel:

> The Lord will give him the throne of David his father. He shall rule over the house of Jacob forever. And his reign will have no end. (*Luke* 1:32-33).

The eschatological joy announced by the prophets finds its realization, then, in a surprising, unexpected way. The Daughter of Sion, ideal personification of Israel, becomes a very distinct person: Miryam, a poor young girl of Galilee, whom God has prepared to be Mother of God in the person of His Son. She is the result of the preparation that God patiently accomplished, by caring for His people for more than two millennia. She, in person, is the new "Ark of the Covenant," a living Ark of the Covenant, within which God will dwell.

She is both the Mother of the expected Messiah and Mother of God, whose coming the prophets had announced. These two lines of prophecy converge, and are realized in her.

The translation, "Hail or Rejoice" would therefore trivialize the marvelous announcement that Mary received and meditated in her heart and which she transmitted through the Evangelist Luke.

The Greeks have always understood this *chaire* as an exceptional, a unique joy. The Greek homilists who paraphrase the Angelical Salutation underline the joy, and this also begins the admirable "Akathistos Hymn," where the praise of Mary begins with these words:

> Rejoice, O bride unbrided.
> Rejoice, by whom gladness will be
> enkindled.
> Rejoice, by whom the curse will be
> quenched.
> Rejoice, ransom of Eve's tears.
> Rejoice, for you are the throne of the King.
> Rejoice, for you bear him who bears all
> things.
> Rejoice, star heralding the sun.
> Rejoice, womb of God's incarnation.
> Rejoice, thou by whom creation is renewed.
> Rejoice, through whom the Creator became a
> babe.
> Rejoice, bride unbrided.

It would be difficult to express joy and exultation any more strongly.

The Latins too have often understood this. While *Ave* (Hail), however poetic it may be, certainly does not reflect the joy of the Greek text, a number of translations and hymns of the Middle Ages prefer to say: *Gaude* (Rejoice).

This discussion on the fuller sense of "Rejoice" (Hebrew: *Ranni;* Greek: *chaire*), is not at all intended to downgrade the Latin translation, which has been sanctified, magnified, haloed by the fervent recitation of so many generations of Christians: trillions and trillions of times.

Ave (Hail) is also a greeting, and the hearts of Christians have come to embue it with all the joy that the original biblical text expressed, just as a "hello," after a long separation is normally filled with warmth and joy.

CHAPTER 2

Mary

The second word of the **Hail Mary** calls upon Mary by name. In the Gospel, this name does not appear right after the Angel's greeting, for the second word of the Annunciation gives another name to Mary, a new name, a name of grace, as we shall see in the next chapter. The Angel Gabriel does in fact call Mary by her name, but only a little later on. (*Luke* 1:30).

When, possessed by the fear of God, she ponders and asks what this greeting means, the Angel addresses her a second time:

Fear not, Mary (Greek: *"Mariam"*; Hebrew: *Miryam*).

This name then is a part of the Angel's message. The **Hail Mary** places it within a new context, separating it from the "do not fear," which would have no place in a prayer addressed to Mary.

Value

It is fitting that we invoke Mary by her name.

In all human communication, it is good to know whom one is speaking to, and better contact is established when a person is called by name.

If a person is in accord with someone, he asks for his name. And people who love one another are happy to call one another by their names. When someone dear to us has gone, we sorely feel the lack of this.

In biblical times the name had a vital, an extraordinary meaning and importance. That is why the revelation of God's name to Moses remains one of the great moments in the Old Testament. Thanks to the revelation of this name, he can invoke God, he acquires a power over His heart, and at the same time a knowledge of His intimate nature: *I am He who is,* the being par excellence. He alone exists of Himself, as compared with creatures, who exist only through Him.

"I am He who is, you are she who is not," as the Lord Himself commented to Catherine of Siena, when lovingly revealing to her His transcendence.

Even today, anonymity creates a gulf, a barrier, while a name brings about a relation, an association. When I was a child, as we were returning one night from Nantes, in our old B-12 Citroën, the automobile broke down on the outskirts of a village. Midnight was approaching. Everyone was asleep. What was to be done? Before knocking at the home of the garage mechanic, whose house was identified by his sign, my father went to the corner bar, the only place with a light on, to ask for the name of the garageman. Why did he waste time to do this?

"It's because this way he will come," my father said.

And he began to call beneath the window: "Monsieur Pivetot!"

The latter, who no doubt had made himself deaf, got up at the sound of his name. The plan succeeded, and the car was repaired.

In a small way, this points out why Moses wanted so much to know the name of God, who knew him by his name. . .

And does not Jesus rise up at the sound of His name, and Mary likewise at the sound of hers?

The Origin

The name of Mary, (in Hebrew: *Miryam*), is not hers alone. We find it already in the Old Testament.

The sister of Moses and Aaron was called Miryam, daughter of Amram and Jochabed of the tribe of Levi. It was she who watched the floating basket coated with pitch, wherein her mother had placed the infant Moses. And when the daughter of Pharaoh came to bathe in the Nile, it was she who intervened to find a nurse—the mother herself (*Exodus* 2:1-10).

Miryam was a prophetess, as will be Mary, the Mother of Jesus. She too composed a song of thanksgiving, transmitted by the Bible. This was after the crossing of the Red Sea. (*Exodus* 15:21).

> *Sing to the Lord, for he has covered himself with*
> *glory. Horse and chariot he has cast into the sea."*

Miryam, by whom Moses had been saved from the waters, glorified God for all his people, saved in their turn from the waters that engulfed the enemy army.

But the sister of Moses is in no way Mary's equal. She was subject to error and to sin. She revolted against Moses when he married a Cushite woman (very likely the Madianite, Sepphora: *Exodus* 2:21). She plotted against him, so that Aaron's word and her own might take over from the faltering leader. But God came to the defense of Moses. Miryam was struck with leprosy, but was cured at the prayer of Moses (*Numbers* 12:1-15; cf. *Deuteronomy* 24:9). She died at Cades (*Numbers* 20:1). The Prophet Micha (6:4) cites her, together with Moses and Aaron, as a guide for Israel in the going forth from Egypt.

Meaning

Does this name have a meaning? Each name has more or less an etymology which means something, and the Greek Church of the first centuries made up names full of meaning:

> Dorothy—gift of God
> Théodulph—servant of God
> Théophile—friend of God
> Philothea—lover of God

The etymology of Miryam is stil in dispute. Seventy different interpretations have been proposed. O. Bardenhewer collected and discussed them. Most are evidently fantasies. Here are the most poetic, the most eloquent, those most frequently cited:

> Star of the sea
> Enlightener (or Illuminated)
> Bitter sea (or Sea of Bitterness: referring to her sorrows)
> Myrrh of the sea
> Lady, Queen (the Latin *Domina*)
> Mother of the Lord

F. Zorell tried to establish the interpretation, "Beloved of God." This is an Egyptian name, he observes, for it is in Egypt that the name Miryam was given to the sister of Moses. In that country, a number of proper names were formed from "Meri," (beloved), joined to the name of a god. G. Roschini supports this explanation because of its doctrinal appropriateness: "This etymology received [from Mary herself] the most simple and most splendid confirmation, for, among all rational creatures, the Blessed Virgin is undoubtedly, from all eternity, the most beloved of God, etc." (*Mariologia* 1947, T. 2, p. 66; cf. *Enciclopedia*

Theotokos. Milan, 1958, no. 749, p. 867).

The most recent exegetes retain the following in preference to others:

— She who sees: (from the Hebrew Ra'ah: to see) and
— Lady, feminine of Lord (O. Odelin and R. Seguineau, *Dictionnaire des noms propres de la Bible.* Paris, DDB, 1978, p. 244).

Testimony of the Magnificat

The *Magnificat* (*Luke* 1:46-55), supports this last solution. Mary's canticle was proclaimed in a semitic tongue, as the great majority of exegetes recognize. When I tried to retranslate it into Hebrew, I was suprised at the ease of the task, for the expressions are totally biblical and Hebraic, rather than Greek.

The greatest surprise in this translation into Hebrew was that it was studded with allusions to the names of persons. The same holds for the *Benedictus* (*Luke* 1:68-79).

Such allusions are a common usage in the Bible. So it is that the root of the name Isaac, found very rarely (only 17 times in the Bible), occurs ten times in the brief sections given to this personage (*Genesis* Chapter 21), with many puns on the word "laugh," which this root signifies.

The same for Joseph, whose case is more complex, for the biblical text plays with several etymologies, to signify that Joseph, sold and cast away by his brothers, brought them together.

When the daughter of Pharaoh adopted the infant found in the Nile, she gave him the name Moses, for, said she, "I have saved him from the waters."

These puns on names are especially frequent in stories about births.

In Luke 1, allusions are especially evident for Zachary, Elizabeth and their son, John the Baptist. The roots of their three names are found together in the first sentence of the *Magnificat* and of the *Benedictus.* The names are formed respectively from the roots:

> Zakar (to remember) for Zachary;
> Shahah (covenant, to take an oath) for Elizabeth;
> Hanan (to have mercy) for John the Baptist.

And the two canticles entwine these three roots in an analogous manner:

> The *Magnificat:*
> *Remembering* (root of the name Zachary),
> *his mercy* (root of the name John),
> *as he swore to Abraham* (Luke says "promised," but the Hebrew substrate was certainly shahah, "to swear").

> The *Benedictus:*
> *to show mercy* (root of the name John) *to our fathers,*
> *and to remember* (root of the name Zachary) *his holy covenant,*
> *oath* (root of the name Elisabeth),
> *which he swore* (same root, a second time) *to Abraham and to our fathers.*

The root of the words "oath," (to swear), softened by the Greek text of the *Magnificat,* is found repeated in the *Benedictus,* in accord with the character of the Hebrew language, where these repetitions re-enforce the meaning. These coincidences, therefore, are not the result of chance.

In this play of allusions, where the name of Jesus (Savior) has not been neglected, it would be surprising if Mary had no part. We find several probable allusions at different levels.

The first words of the *Magnificat: "My soul glorifies the*

Lord (in Greek megalunei)," corresponds to the Hebrew root rum, which means to raise, exalt, carry towards the height. The allusion would be significant. It is, however, confirmed, for the Canticle of Anna, model of Mary's canticle, also employs the same root rum, in the first verse: *"In my God is my strength lifted up."*

Mary's name then seems to mean that she is magnified, raised up by God in her very poverty, indeed because of this poverty, as Mary herself specifies in the remainder of the canticle:

> *The Lord has looked upon the lowliness of his handmaid. Henceforth all generations will call me blessed. (Luke 1:48).*

This lifting up of the poor is the very theme of the first part of the *Magnificat,* in fact, of the entire gospel: God puts down the proud and exalts the lowly. This glory which was Mary's, she herself proclaims for all the poor:

> *He has put down the mighty from their thrones, And has lifted up the lowly. (Luke 1:52).*

Mary's name, then, signifies this exaltation, this lordship of the poor, which is the very essence of the Gospel. Such is the meaning which the name of Mary acquires in the original semitic text, "Domina," which we translate as "Our Lady." Such was the meaning perceived by the Judeo-Christian community of Jerusalem, through whom this canticle of the Mother of the Lord was transmitted to the evangelist Luke.

The Name of Jesus

In the semitic language (probably Hebrew, the liturgical language), the name of Jesus appeared, at the very outset, associated with that of Mary:

> *My soul glorifies the Lord and my spirit rejoices*
> *in God my Savior.*

In Hebrew, "my Savior" and "my Jesus" are the same thing. And that is why St. Jerome, translating *Habacuc* 3:18 (of which the second line of the *Magnificat* is an echo), translated it as: "I rejoice in God my Jesus."

Perhaps these puns surprise us and strike us as subtle. They are common in a culture where names have meaning. The importance of each name and of its meaning holds a special place; hence the interest in this etymology shown in the beautiful canticle of Mary, one of the first prayers of the early Church.

Whatever its etymology, today as yesterday, we love the name of somebody whom we love. We pronounce it with joy. Many Christians are sensitive to the name Jesus, a human forename predestined for the Son of God, whose name is above every other name. And so we have the Jesus Prayer, which consists in repeating this name countless times...with results.

The Name of Mary

Many Christians are equally sensitive to the name of Mary, which at one time was the object of a feast.

Alphonse Ratisbonne, who had been converted, suddenly and completely when Mary appeared to him, took this name at his baptism (incongruously since it is a feminine name). He justified this, saying, "If I were to tell you the story of my conversion, one word alone would suffice: Mary." (Alphonese Ratisbonne to C. E. Desgenettes.) And many years later, looking forward to his death, he would say:

"When I am very ill, just speak one word to me: Mary." (*Annales de Notre-Dame de Sion,* June 1884, no. 29, p. 19.)

The Annunciation to Mary
Luke 1:26-38

The angel Gabriel was sent from God to a city of Galilee named Nazareth, to a virgin betrothed to a man whose name was Joseph, of the house of David; and the virgin's name was Mary. And he came to her and said, "Hail, full of grace, the Lord is with you!" But she was greatly troubled at the saying, and considered in her mind what sort of greeting this might be. And the angel said to her, "Do not be afraid, Mary, for you have found favor with God. And behold, you will conceive in your womb and bear a son, and you shall call his name, Jesus.

He will be great, and will be called the Son of the Most High; and the Lord God will give to him the throne of his father David, and he will reign over the house of Jacob forever; and of his kingdom there will be no end."

And Mary said to the angel, "How can this be, since I do not know man?"

And the angel said to her, "The Holy Spirit will come upon you, and the power of the Most High will overshadow you; therefore the child to be born will be called holy, the Son of God. And behold, your kinswoman Elizabeth in her old age has also conceived a son; and this is the sixth month with her who was called barren. For with God nothing will be impossible."

And Mary said, "Behold, I am the handmaid of the Lord; let it be done to me according to your word." And the angel departed from her.

CHAPTER 3

Full of Grace

The next three words of the **Hail Mary** are a translation of a Greek word that is untranslatable: "kecharitómené."

This is the perfect passive participle of the verb "charitoó," where we see the root "charis," which means grace, the gratuitousness of God. Sometimes this has been diminished to "pardoned," or "pleasing," but the word means much more: "She who is the object of the grace of God, of His favor, of His love."

And the love of God has the creative capacity to render good that which it loves.

The verb "charitoó" is well chosen to signify this, for in contrast with the verb "charizomai" (as St. John Chrysostom observed), verbs ending in oó signify a transformation. Thus "leukoó" means to make white, "douloó" to make a slave. Mary then is transformed by grace in accord with God's predilection.

The verb is used in the perfect tense. It therefore signifies a lasting grace. The outstanding Hellenist Osty paraphrases as follows: "You who have been, and remain, object of the favor of God."

Finally, this title was given to Mary as a new name, one that explains God's designs for her. Throughout the Bible, from Abraham, father of the faith, to Peter, first of the Apostles and foundation of the Church, God renames those whom he chooses for a mission of great importance.

The angel begins by giving Mary a name of grace. Miryam was the name that her parents had lovingly chosen for their child.

"Full of grace," full of love, is the name which God himself gives no less lovingly through the voice of the angel.

With happiness let us repeat this name and this praise, aware that our tongue and our spirit are incapable of sounding the depths of its divine significance.

CHAPTER 4

The Lord is With You

The Lord is with you. (*Luke* 1:28). These words complete the praise which the Angel Gabriel addresses to Mary from God. They give the reason for it Mary can rejoice, she is filled with grace, for the Lord is with her: without any restriction, without diminution, from the beginning, since she has been preserved from original sin.

Not only has the Lord loved her with a love of predilection, but, for her part, she has not placed any obstacle to His love. She responded to it without fail, love for love, with a marvelous enthusiasm, prompted by the Holy Spirit.

This enables her to contribute to the new and mysterious grace that will change the face of the earth. She who is with God is going to give birth to God, not only in her heart (as every believer), but in her body; at first in her heart, then in her body, according to the expression of the Church Fathers adopted by the Council:

> "By faith, Mary conceived Christ in her heart before doing so in her body." (*Constitution Lumen gentium,* no. 53.)

God can be born among men only in and by faith. Mary is not a robot, nor a surrogate mother as some have stupidly asserted. She is the one who loved God and desired His coming on earth to the point of becoming His mother according to nature. She is truly His mother. She gave birth to Him just as any other mother does.

The Swiss theologian, Aloïs Müller, went so far as to say: "According to the Fathers, Mary is the ultimate instance where perfect faith brings to birth the Son of God Himself, not just spiritually but corporally." The Incarnation is the supreme realization of the mystery of faith. Mary is the fulfillment and the summit of faith. Thus, she becomes at one and the same time, the Mother of the Son of God and the first one who adhered to Him in faith: the prototype of the Church.

These words of the Angel's greeting, *The Lord is with you,* introduce some expressions that are more precise: the "with you" will become "in you, in your womb." We have here an echo of the prophecy of Zephaniah (3:14-18) as we have already seen.

The Lord is with you—and so with all. This is both the first and last word of the Gospel of Matthew.

— His very first chapter (on the Infancy), announces Jesus as Emmanuel, that is to say God-with-us. (*Matthew* 1:23).
— And the last verse of his entire gospel ends with the final words of Jesus Himself: *I-am-with-you all days until the end of the world.* (*Matthew* 28:20).

Like the priest, Zachary, Mary is troubled by the first words of the Annunciation. But he is troubled by the sight of the Angel (*Luke* 1:12); and Mary at what she heard (1:29). The text does not say that she saw the angel.

What troubles Mary is the very import of the message: the announcement of eschatological joy, that name of grace which God gives her, and this alliance with Him implied by the very simple expression: *"The Lord is with you."*

Mary begins to reflect in order to understand what this

greeting means. (*Luke* 1:29). Her reflection is a dialogue with God. Here too, there is a contrast with Zachary. Fear "falls upon him." (*Luke* 1:12). He is dumbfounded, passive. But Mary remains active, for mature reflection. Luke's gospel gives life to the notion claiming that the Church reserves activity to men and restricts women to passivity. Quite the contrary is true.

The angel reassures her (in the same terms as Zachary):

— *Fear not, Mary.*

But he adds:

— *You have found grace with God.* (*Luke* 1:30).

These last words are like a commentary and an explanation of the name of grace with which he as God's messenger had greeted her (formed from the word *charis*—grace), a divine explanation and confirmation of the name given from on high.

Then he comes to the decisive part of the message:

— *Behold, you shall conceive in your womb and bear a son: He shall be great, he shall be called Son of the Most High.*

This verse is startling. The son whom Mary is going to bear in her flesh is the Son of the Most High. The Son of God is going to become the son of Mary. The angel gives this transcendent title before speaking of the heir of David. (*Luke* 1:33).

With a mysterious realism, the message underlines both the fleshly reality of this birth and also the transcendence of the Son. He is great, in an absolute way, without restriction (God alone is great), and Son of the Most High. That is what He is, was, and always will be.

It is then, in an extraordinary way, that the Lord is with

her—as her son. Her new alliance with God is a maternity that integrated God into the very fabric of the human race, of human history, of the human family.

It is only after having declared this divine filiation that the angel considers the Messiah's descent from David (*Luke* 1:33), for he is Messiah much more as the Son of the Most High, than as the son of David.

Here again Mary reflects. This is something she does not understand. This Creator God has given her a liberty which never acts haphazardly. It is always careful to adhere to God and to be transparent to Him.

From the beginning, filled with love for Him alone, she at an early age had understood in her heart (as has been the case with some other young children) that she belonged totally to God, and would always belong only to Him. She had renounced sexual fulfillment and maternity. God himself had inspired this in her. She had already faced the problem: How can this be reconciled with the marriage plans that the family had formed with Joseph, in accord with the customs of that time—and of ours as well until recently—where the parents had the initiative and a decisive role in the marriage of their children?

If God had asked in her heart that she be His alone, how could He now ask that she be a mother, even if hers were to be a glorious maternity? She asks:

— *How shall this be, since I do not know man.* (*Luke* 1:34).

This question in the present tense signifies a resolve, a state of being, as when someone says: I do not drink, I do not smoke. She had been engaged to Joseph in conditions we do not know of. We know only that this family's decision had not shaken her decision of never "knowing man" in the biblical sense; that is, according to the sexual meaning of the words, found at the very beginning of Genesis (*Genesis* 4:1, 17, 25).

The angel had not accepted Zachary's objections at the announcement of the birth of John the Baptist:

— *How shall I know this, for I am an old man, and my wife is advanced in years.* (*Luke* 1:18).

The priest, accustomed to exercising authority, seems to be asking for verification and proofs. The angel silenced him:

> *Behold you shall be dumb, not being able to speak until the day when these things shall come to pass, because you did not believe my words which shall be fulfilled in their time.* (*Luke* 1:20).

With Mary, it is different. She asks for clarification respecting two apparently contradictory demands, both of which come from God. God always appealed to her freedom, her lucidity. She seeks to understand His will. The woman filled with grace, soon to be mother of the Savior, has the right to an answer. In clear contrast with Zachary, she will be prophetically lauded for her faith:

— *Blessed are you who have believed, for the words spoken to you from the Lord will be fulfilled.* (*Luke* 1:45).

Here we see the opposite of the familiar expression: Let women be silent in the Church. Zachary, in the exercise of the highest priestly functions, is reprimanded for having spoken. Let the priest be silent in the Church. And Mary has the right to speak.

The angel answers by confirming that the Son of God, her son, will come to her from God alone. For that he uses expressions that she can understand, the words of the Bible that tell of God's coming upon the Ark of the Covenant, to announce a new era:

Exodus 40:35	Luke 1:35
God's coming upon the Ark of the Covenant	God's coming upon Mary
The cloud with its shadow covered the tabernacle, the glory of Yahweh filled the dwelling	*The power of the Most High will overshadow you. Therefore the child to be born will be called holy, Son of God.*

In the desert, the luminous cloud had come to cover the Ark of the Covenant, while the glory of God filled it and it shone with glory. The cloud, which hovered above the Ark of the Covenant, signified the transcendence of God. The presence within the Ark signified his immanence.

For Mary, God's transcendence, i.e., the shadow of the "Shekinah," is expressed in the same way, but his immanence is manifested in a new manner, different, one never before heard of: not merely an effulgence of glory, but the humble dwelling within her of the Holy One (God alone is holy, says the Bible), of the Son of God. (*Luke* 1:35).

In Mary, the promise of the prophets is realized in a manner which surpasses all expectation. She is going to bring forth not only a Messiah, but God Himself. The obscure hopes evoked by the prophets are realized in her through this maternity in a way that is perfect, concrete and familiar.

An Annoucement Addressed to Us

The marvel that the Lord brings about in Mary does not make her a distant princess. If God is with her, if God is in her, it is to live in solidarity with a world of sinners, to be immersed in this world, in order to save it.

That which Mary received is given to her, not for herself, but for all of us. What she initiates will be shared. She has been filled with joy so that all might receive this same joy—the announcement of the Good News. She was filled with grace so that others might be filled with it. The Lord is with her in order to be with us. He comes to dwell within her in order to dwell within us: through the indwelling of grace, through the Eucharist, where we receive His very body, just as Mary did, thanks to Mary who formed that body.

The mystery of the Annunciation, which the first words of the angel bring about, is presented not only to be admired but to be imitated.

The alliance with God, offered to Mary, is offered to us as well. It is an invitation to do as she did: to open our heart to the Lord by faith and charity, so that He will be with us, in us.

Is He? Yes, on His part. The Creator does not cease to love us, to create us. But do we welcome Him? Does our response in some small way resemble that of Mary? Does our ardor for God correspond to His ardent love for us?

If we are still far from it, let us ardently ask for this grace from the Holy Spirit, the fountain of life placed within us by baptism. The era of God's wonders has not come to an end.

Mary has introduced us into a new world, where God is truly with us, in us. This changes everything. And we can learn how to live with Him, following in Mary's steps, prototype and model of the Church.

Context of the Visitation
"Blessed are you among women."
Luke 1:39-56

During those days Mary set out and traveled to the hill country in haste to a town of Judah, where she entered the house of Zechariah and greeted Elizabeth. When Elizabeth heard Mary's greeting, the infant leaped in her womb, and Elizabeth, filled with the holy Spirit, cried out in a loud voice and said, "Most blessed are you among women, and blessed is the fruit of your womb. And how does this happen to me, that the mother of my Lord should come to me? For at the moment the sound of your greeting reached my ears, the infant in my womb leaped for joy. Blessed are you who believed that what was spoken to you by the Lord would be fulfilled."

And Mary said: "My soul proclaims the greatness of the Lord; my spirit rejoices in God my savior. For he has looked upon his handmaid's lowliness; behold, from now on will all ages call me blessed. The Mighty One has done great things for me, and holy is his name. His mercy is from age to age to those who fear him. He has shown might with his arm, dispersed the arrogant of mind and heart. He has thrown down the rulers from their thrones but lifted up the lowly. The hungry he has filled with good things; the rich he has sent away empty. He has helped Israel his servant, remembering his mercy, according to his promise to our fathers, to Abraham and to his descendants forever."

Mary remained with her about three months and then returned to her home.

CHAPTER 5

Elizabeth's Prophecy: "Blessed are you among Women and Blessed is the Fruit of your Womb"

The next part of the **Hail Mary** no longer makes use of the angel's words, but those of Elizabeth, when she greets Mary in her home at Ain Karim, near Jerusalem:

> *"Blessed are you among women and blessed is the fruit of your womb." (Luke* 1:42).

This act of praise also has a history. The Gospel recounts it in the same first chapter of Luke, at the time of the Visitation. Let us place it in context.

Filled With God Alone

Mary has received an extraordinary message: *Behold you shall conceive in your womb and bear a son. You will give him the name Jesus. (Luke* 1:31).

Then she learned some other extraordinary news:

— The son promised to her is the *"Son of the Most High"* (*Luke* 1:32): the Son of God is going to become her son. The Son of God coming to earth will also be the heir promised to David, though Luke does not explain how.

Thus, there come together two great prophetic lines of the Old Testament, lines that appeared divergent and incompatible.

— *It is the Messiah-King, descendant of David, Who will come to reign;*

— *It is God Himself, Who will reign over His people and over all the people of the earth.*

Mary was not able to understand the convergence of these two prophecies.

— Is it God Himself Who would come, or rather a man born among men? And how would He be born without rescinding the decision to remain a virgin with which He had inspired her?

— This child, the angel had announced, would come from God alone, from the Holy Spirit, from the power of the Most High. He will be God Himself: He will be called Holy, Son of God.

By the light of the Old Testament, Mary was thus initiated, in her heart and in her mind, into the mystery of the Incarnation, which is at one and the same time the eschatological reign of God and the reign of the Messiah. It is one and the same, for God and the Messiah are one and the same. The virginal birth will be a miraculous sign of His Divine transcendence.

After that, the Angel who had refused to give the sign asked for by Zachary, the priest, freely gives a sign to Mary, who did not ask for any. Her cousin Elizabeth, wife of the priest Zachary, has been freed from the sterility which had made her an object of reproach. (*Luke* 1:25). She is going to become the mother of the precursor:

> *And behold your cousin Elizabeth has conceived a son in her old age. She is in her sixth month,*

she who has been called sterile. For nothing is im-
possible with God. (Luke 1:36).

Mary overwhelmed by the angel's answer receives this
additional unexpected sign. For God did not want to enter
her by way of surprise but with her full knowledge. God
the Creator is not a tyrant who coerces. He has created
men's very liberty: *"Then left them free to make their own*
decisions," as Scripture says. (*Ecclesiasticus* 15:14). He does
not constrain this liberty. He respects it and carries it into
effect. God does not come to Mary by making a forced
entry, by some kind of ravishing, as men might do (which
is what some theologians imagine, theologians who have
badly understood the biblical text or who have distorted
its meaning). He awaits Mary's consent to His love and
He awaits our own. Mary gives hers with a new ardor,
without restriction, forever, and irreversibly:
Behold the handmaid of the Lord, let it be done to me
as you say.
It is here that the Incarnation begins.
"And the Word was made flesh and lived among us," as
John makes explicit (1:14).
These words conclude the Angelus whose first two ver-
sicles were taken from the Gospel of the Annunciation (*Luke*
1:28-32, 38).

Mary has become the new tabernacle of God, a living
tabernacle. This grace enraptures her. She who had
renounced having children (she would have loved to have
children and renounced having any for the sake of God
alone) now has a son. She carries within her this child
whom she is going to form. And she is filled with him
as, humanly speaking, so many women are who desire
and await a son.
But this son is not only her son, He is *"the Son of the*

Most High" (*Luke* 1:32), the *"Son of God"* (1:35) revealed to her by the angel.

It would seem that nothing more remains for her but to savor the mystery of this extraordinary gift. God lives in her. He has pervaded, transported, placed within her His being of glory and light. The Son, eternal image of the Father, also becomes His human image, thanks to Mary. Like every mother, she forms this image according to her own likeness. She could meditate on that for an eternity.

Sharing

But something else takes hold of her and impels her. She cannot save this for herself. She must share it. With whom? For this is the incomprehensible secret of God!

With her old cousin Elizabeth, to whom the last words of the angel seemed to send her: *"and behold, your cousin Elizabeth has conceived, she too has a son in her old age."* (Luke 1:37).

Mary departs for the distant home of her old cousin. She leaves in haste, the Gospel says (1:39). It is quite far, more than a hundred kilometers along tortuous roads, that are rough and not very safe. For the wife of the priest Zachary lives in the "hill country of Judea" near the Temple, very likely in the little neighboring village of Ain-Karim (four kilometers from Jerusalem).

Mary's Pentecost

Mary has just been the first one to receive this announcement:

The Holy Spirit will come upon you. (*Luke* 1:35).

Just as the apostles will much later receive Christ's announcement:

The Holy Spirit will come upon you. (*Acts* 1:8).

Mary experiences the very first Pentecost, and her Pentecost opens the way to all the others. Does she understand this?

She is well acquainted with the feast of Pentecost as it existed in Israel. This is the celebration of God's alliance in the desert with Moses and his people. The Prophet Ezechiel (34:25; and 37:26) announced a new alliance (which she also knows): the law of God would be engraved on their hearts by the Holy Spirit. (*Ezechiel* 36:26; cf. 37:5). She has already experienced that interior law. As yet she has no idea of the new Pentecost that will come upon the future Church within thirty-three years, after the death and resurrection of Christ, when the Holy Spirit will come upon the twelve apostles and the 120 disciples, united with her in the upper room in Jerusalem. But the proto-Pentecost which the angel has just announced to her: *"The Holy Spirit will come upon you,"* fills her heart and her maternal womb and all her being, which the Son of God now inhabits.

Of course, from the time of her Immaculate Conception she has been filled with the Holy Spirit. But that implicit gift had not yet been revealed.

Then too, one is never finished with the Holy Spirit. With him, we go from plenitude to plenitude. At Pentecost (ten days after the Ascension of Christ), the apostles will be filled with the Holy Spirit (*Acts* 2:4), but they will be filled with him anew. (*Acts* 4:31). For what purpose?, one might ask. This had already taken place. Yes, but they now receive a new plenitude, in order to face persecution. And in the same way, Mary will go from plenitude to plenitude.

So then, it is the new fullness of the Annunciation that Mary (filled with the Holy Spirit and filled with Christ) is going to share with her cousin Elizabeth. Mary's journey brings her son, the Messiah, very close to Jerusalem, the place where He will reign. It brings the Son of God to the proximity of the Temple, that Herod is beginning to rebuild.

It is a long road through the mountains, a rocky and dangerous road.

Many centuries later, in the middle of the nineteenth, it was still a hazardous road. Alphonse Ratisbonne, although a good horseman, had a bad fall because of some falling rocks. He would suffer some effect from it for the rest of his life. The journey took about a week.

Elizabeth's Pentecost

Mary joyfully greets her cousin. Here we see the happiness of a familial and friendly meeting, enriched by the double grace that two women share. During this visit, a new spark from the Holy Spirit will be ignited between the two women, and between the Son of God and His precursor.

Scarecely had the sound of Mary's voice reached the ears of Elizabeth when she was filled with the Holy Spirit. (*Luke* 1:40). The Old Testament had met the New Testament.

The First Prophecy of the New Testament

And at once she makes a prophecy about the glory of her cousin: *"Blessed are you among women and blessed is the fruit of your womb!"* (*Luke* 1:42).

This is how the words we repeat in the **Hail Mary** sprung forth some 2,000 years ago. The prophecy continues with the words:

> *"How does this happen to me that the Mother of my Lord should come to me?"* (She recognizes Mary as "Mother of the Lord"), *"for, behold, at the sound of your voice the infant leaped in my womb with joy!"* (*Luke* 1:43-44).

Elizabeth perceived that the stirring of her child was like a dance, like David's dance before the ark. (*2 Samuel* 6:5, 14, 21).

The expression (which the official text does not dare to translate) is correct in every respect. Today we can film the movements of a little child within its mother's womb, the first joyful expression it makes of its vital energy in that warm nest where is rests secure. A doctor in an American abortion clinic had filmed this dance of the embryos and then, when he filmed the panic-stricken reactions of the little one facing the machine that would cut him up, he broke away completely and became a promoter for repealing a murderous law. The dance of the little ones on the threshold of their existence had spoken.

For John the Baptist, according to the prophecy of his mother, this dance within the womb is already a prophetic act: the first expression, silent and non-rational, of his mission as Precursor, his first meeting with the Lord.

Elizabeth concludes with this praise of Mary:

> *Blessed is she who has believed, that what was spoken to her by the Lord would be fulfilled.* (*Luke* 1:45).

The first words spoken by Elizabeth, which we repeat in the **Hail Mary,** may surprise us. To a rigid theocentrism it would seem that they are uttered in reverse:

First Mary: *"Blessed are you among women."*

Then Jesus: *"And blessed is the fruit of your womb."*

Should not Jesus be declared blessed first?

The word order is explained by the biblical allusions in the Visitation, to the account of the transfer of the Ark of the Covenant to Jerusalem in *2 Samuel* 6.

The Ark had been kept *"in the houe of Obededom (2 Samuel* 6:9), just as Mary *"in the house of Zachary."* (*Luke*

1:40). She, like the Ark, also remained there *"three months."* (*1 Samuel* 6:11, and *Luke* 1:56).

David fears (just as Mary does in *Luke* 1:30), and this fear inspires in him those words which Elizabeth curiously enough adopts in the text being discussed:

Cry of David (*2 Samuel* 6:9)	Cry of Elizabeth (*Luke* 1:43)
Whence is this to me that the Ark of the Lord should enter my house	How does this happen to me that the Mother of my Lord should come to me!

Then too, Elizabeth names Mary first *(Blessed are you among women),* for it is Mary who comes to her visibly, and it is Mary who greets and embraces her. The child, whom she does not know, remains mysteriously hidden within his mother, and it is through Mary that Elizabeth begins to surmise his reality, prophetically. She mentions the mother before the child, for the child comes through his mother, who alone can be seen, and who brings him to her. She does not know the Lord except through the Mother of the Lord.

Her praise then is of an ascending order. Elizabeth moves gradually from the mother, who is visible, to the invisible Child. And the entire account of the Visitation (like that of the Annunciation), explains step by step the profound unity of mother and child—for Mary as for Elizabeth. We have here a complete theology of the maternal womb, which some theologians of the Third World are beginning to discern, as for example, the Protestant Choan-Seng Song (*The Third Eye Theology.* New York, 1979, Chap. 6, pp. 124-140).

The Name of Jesus

The Church accentuates this biblical praise (*Luke* 1:42), by adding the name of Jesus. This is the last word of the

Latin **Hail Mary:** *fructus ventris tui,* as also of the Italian and English translations. The French prefers to place the name higher up: "and Jesus, the fruit of your womb is blessed." Perhaps this is better literarily and euphonically, but unfortunately the word loses the force it would have as a conclusion and organ point.

The name of Jesus, that Mary had been commissioned to give to the Christ, certainly has its place in the **Hail Mary.** It is full of meaning. Mary had understood its obvious significance, and the first words of her song of thanksgiving, the *Magnificat,* allude to it.

> "My soul magnifies the Lord and my spirit rejoices in God my Savior. (*Luke* 1:46-47).

God my Savior and God my Jesus mean the same thing in Hebrew as we have seen.

Thanksgiving

Mary's song completes the account of the Visitation.

After Elizabeth, Mary in her turn prophesies, and it is to render back to God all the praise that Elizabeth had given her from God, for all that comes from God is completed by returning to God. Every grace must end in an act of thanksgiving. And in giving thanks we do not lose the grace received but complete it. This is what Mary does in thanking God for having filled her very poverty:

> "For he has regarded the lowliness of his handmaid." (*Luke* 1:47).

Mary gives thanks first of all for herself. She has just received the grace of all graces. God became man in her. Then to make known afterwards that God provides, that he has already extended this grace to all the poor, she adds:

*He has deposed the mighty from their thrones
and lifted up the lowly. He has filled the hungry
with good things, and sent away the rich empty.*

Finally, Mary extends her thanksgiving to the distant past as well as to the future and to the entire people of God:

*God has come to the help of his servant Israel
mindful of his mercy, as he promised to our fathers,
to Abraham and his descendants forever.*

The **Hail Mary,** which ends here with the first sentence of Elizabeth's act of thanksgiving, is heavy with the totality of Mary's thanksgiving, which is also ours. For, let us repeat, the initial grace that she received, she received that it be communicated to all. The Visitation is but its first manifestation. Mary also visits us today. Let us be attentive to her. Let us cultivate within ourselves this presence of Mary.

Part II

The Teachings from the Church

CHAPTER 6

Holy Mary

The invocation *Holy Mary,* which begins the second half of the **Hail Mary** comes from some litanies initiated in the seventh century. There, Mary is invoked as the head of all the saints: *Sancta Maria, ora pro nobis.* "Holy Mary, pray for us."

The invocation begins with the word "holy," for Mary is the most holy of all the saints. All the others are, in fact, sinners, sanctified by God as we are. To reach holiness they have had to get rid of the sin that dwelt in them.

"The just man sins seven times a day," says the Book of Proverbs (24:16). This paradox expresses a truth: Much closer to God and to His light, the saints have a better perception of their sins, while we ourselves are often unaware of our own. But their failures, their lack of love are no longer either revolt, lukewarmness, or infractions. They are weaknesses of human frailty, their shadows facing the pure light of God.

Perfect Holiness

Mary alone was holy with a holiness without shadow. This was required for her mission as Mother of God. For if the Son of God came among sinners, for sinners, if He took upon Himself the burden of the world's sins, sin could not penetrate within Him. It could wound, even kill His body, weight down His spirit, but could not contaminate His thrice holy being. She who formed His human nature had to be without stain.

Mary then was preserved from sin. Pius IX defined this truth after long and laborious debates that lasted for centuries: from the twelfth to the nineteenth. This was the dogma of the "Immaculate Conception." Unfortunately, Pius IX's infallible definition, couched in nineteenth-century Latin—a definition that they do not accept, offended the non-Catholic Orientals. And the vision of Mary as all holy, all pure, which our Latin world derived from their ancient tradition, has been obscured for them.

Despite the confusion of age-long controversies, Pius IX recognized in Christian tradition and in the faith of the people of God, that this truth was compelling and that the time had come to authenticate Mary's original grace: her unique vocation as Mother of God implied not merely a purification, but a preservation from sin.

Does this mean that Mary had no need of salvation, that she would not have been redeemed by Christ? Quite the contrary, Pius IX defined correlatively that she was redeemed by anticipation, "in view of the merits of Christ."

This anticipation is the masterpiece of redeeming love, for if the mercy of God performs a marvelous work in purifying from sin, it shows even more marvelous power when at the dawn of salvation, it forestalls and rules out sin from the one who is going to be the sanctuary of God, his mother. This mystery then teaches us the preventive marvels of grace.

Parents and educators have some idea of this. They know how to correct a child's defects, seeking above all to forestall evil. So too, the best medicine is one that prevents the malady in the first place. This latter medicine is more beneficial than remedies and surgery that cure (not without shock, not without after-effects) the sickness once it has been contracted. In the spiritual life as in medicine, let us ask Christ, the physician of souls, for preventive medicines that keep us from falling into sin. He loves to grant this benefit, precious on many levels.

"Lead us not into temptation," the **Our Father** implores.

If then Mary's grace is unique in one sense, it is also exemplary, for, throughout our life, God urges us to avoid evil rather than repair it after a fall. Here again, Mary's perfection is a perfect prototype, not so far removed as we might be tempted to think, and we can imitate her better than appears to be the case.

Merciful Holiness

This exceptional grace makes of Mary a distant princess, unable to understand us who are sinners. It removes her from human solidarity, as certain of the Orthodox have objected to me.

This objection is illusory, for sin is never a means to understanding. We do not understand sin through sin. A sinner can be the accomplice of another sinner. He is not truly his friend. And often we look with horror at those who have the same fault as we do. We perceive them as insupportable caricatures, as an offensive mirror or a living accusation.

We do not understand sin through sin but through love, and God gave Mary the fullness of love necessary to become the mother of sinners in Him, our Savior.

When we pray to Mary, let us then give this word **holy** its full significance. It establishes and measures our confidence. Mary is the link between the holiness of God and us sinners. This prepares the way for the rest of the **Hail Mary** where we supplicate.

Of course when we recite the very dense words of the **Hail Mary** in the ordinary rhythm of human speech, we are unable to perceive their profoundness and density. And this can invite us to another form of prayer, a complimentary one, the meditated recitation of the **Hail Mary,** when we have the time or during our sleepless nights.

Prayer of the Heart

At Medjugorje, in June 1988, some Americans asked the seer Ivan, "How long does it take you to recite your rosary?"

"Two hours," he answered.

Some antagonists who were there to trap him in his speech, derided him. In fact, when he says the rosary by himself, he does it with the prayer of the heart, stopping at each word so that he grasps its whole extent, all its truth, that it may truly insert itself in him, penetrate him. And then while the recitation lasts, it is more than a recitation, it is a contemplation, an effusion, a transparent communion.

A former drug addict, rehabilitated at Medjugorje, who would zealously rattle off rosary after rosary, recently learned the secret of a more profound prayer from Ivan. He said, "Ivan always used to tell me, 'You do not pray enough with the heart.' I did not understand what he meant. Then one day it came to me. I stopped at each word. It was as if gold were flowing."

CHAPTER 7

Mother of God

The invocation *Holy Mary* is followed by the paradoxical title which places her at the summit of creation and raises her above the angels: Mother of God.

A Paradoxical and Much Disputed Title

This title may appear to be an exaggeration. Mary did not engender God as such. The Eternal existed before this mere creature, who came at the end of the ages. She only gave birth, just as any other mother, to a man, whose body she formed and who was truly a man like any other, with two eyes, two arms and two legs, with his feebleness, his tears, his imperious appetite for nourishment, and that thirst for the love which he expects in the caresses and the smile of his mother.

In short, she did nothing else but give birth in time and in human history to the humanity assumed by the Son of God that He might live in solidarity among us and save us from within.

In the fifth century, the Patriarch of Constantinople, Nestorius, penetrated by these considerations, believed that he had to fight against the title, Mother of God.

"Let us call her mother of the man Jesus *(Anthropotokos)*, or Mother of Christ *(Christotokos)*, but not *Theotokos*." This

45

term had its provoking side. Literally it means: She who was delivered of God.

It is true that Mary only engendered the man in Jesus Christ. She did for Him what all human mothers do. It is then with respect to His humanity that she is mother of the Son of God. This must be clearly understood to avoid any ambiguity and all idolatry. She causes the Son of God to be born in human history. She is His historic mother.

But this human truth about Mary's maternity does not say everything. It deliniates its means and its development but not its profound essence: for maternity is essentially a relation of mother to son. This personal link gives Mary a unique relation to the person of the Son of God, fundamentally a relation of love and a dignity without equal.

This is why the Church reacted vigorously against the Patriarch Nestorius, who condemned the title *Theotokos*. The bishops, united in ecumenical council, deposed him even though he was the first of the Eastern bishops, bishop of the capital city. This took place at Ephesus in 431. Some delegates there represented the Pope.

Mary is Certainly Not a Goddess

"Fanaticism, idolatry," some will say. "Do they really want to make a goddess of Mary? Do these bishops and these people miss the pagan goddesses that had been dethroned?"

In no way. Pagan goddesses had no standing in the eyes of Christians. For them, these apotheoses of natural forces were outdated myths. They held them in horror. Mary is neither Venus, nor Aphrodite, goddess of love, nor any other. They were not tempted to foist upon Mary these unreal and perverse images. We have here something entirely different, something foreign to the culture of the time and necessary to express the unheard of innovation coming from Christian revelation.

A Truth Divine and Human

The title, "Mother of God," already widely known for more than a century at the time of the Council of Ephesus, was doubly significant for an authentic knowledge both of God and of humanity. (Today we would say for both theology and anthropology.)

1. The title, "Mother of God," has some importance for Christian anthropology, for to deny that Mary is Mother of God would be to fail to appreciate the humanity upon which God has bestowed astonishing privileges, such as the angels do not have at all. The angels are far superior to us in nature, in intelligence, in power, but they cannot give birth to beings like themselves. In this too, man has been created in a very special way according to God's image: he can engender, as God does. We must understand well this privilege and mystery which honors humanity.

Maternity and fatherhood are not defined by the making of a "product," as we say nowadays, but by the personal relation of father and mother to the new human person they have made and whose soul God has created. In conceiving a child, father and mother engage the creative act of God. They cooperate with Him to form the living organism wherein this person will assume a body and under their guidance will awaken to the human capacity for knowledge and love. God gives to the little one a soul which forms, directs, and governs the body, but transcends it: an immortal soul that will survive it.

Maternity and fatherhood then are not constituted by what a father and mother furnish of the material and biological, by their "product." Otherwise we would have to say (in an awkward way) that the mother is mother of the ovum and that the father is father of the spermatozoa. No, father and mother together are (and they know this well) mother and father forever of the person of their child: Monica, or Peter, or Jacqueline, or Paul.

Mary too is the mother of the person of her child: Jesus. Now Jesus is God in person. Mary is then Mother of God, Mother of the second person of the Trinity, who is absolutely God. To deny this, one would do away with the dignity not alone of Mary but of every mother. It would be an insult to humanity.[1]

2. But to contest that Mary is Mother of God would be still more serious on the theological plane: it would deny the personal and divine unity of Christ, and for the same reason it would deny human salvation. This was the line taken by the Council of Ephesus. It was not a Mariological council, as legend would have it, but a Christological one: a reaction against those who were sundering the two persons of Jesus by dissociating God and man.

For the Greeks the temptation to do this was great, for they were fascinated by the immutable transcendence of God. They had perceived Him with a beautiful philosophical profundity. They were careful to remove from Him every degrading contact with the vicissitudes of this world. Thus they were tempted to separate as much as possible:

— the Son of God: transcendant, eternal, incorruptible and
— the man Jesus, born of Mary, subject to suffering and death.

---

1. Father and mother have this privilege of being cocreators with God "from whom every paternity [and maternity] takes its name in Heaven and on earth." (*Ephesians* 3:15). Human fatherhood and maternity are then a human participation in the transcendent and universal fatherhood of God.

But then God and man would become two entities, two different persons. In this perspective (however profound their union), we could no longer say that God in person was born, suffered and died for us. God's solidarity with man, through the Incarnation of the Son of God, would disappear. The love of God, who brought about the folly of sharing the human condition, would be misunderstood, mutilated, denied. The Son of God would not have gone to give "the greatest proof of love: to give his life for the one he loves." (*John* 15:13). He would only have mimed this through His human double. It is this that the Council of Ephesus reacted against: not to rehabilitate the title "Mother of God," but to safeguard the personal unity of Christ: God made man.

This was essential for the "admirable exchange" whereby God became man in order to divinize mankind. Mary was chosen to bring about this exchange by engendering the Son of God on earth. Thus by God's choice, she became Mother of God for the salvation of mankind. Luther recognized this unmistakable dignity as well as the virginity required for this primordial maternity.

So the subtle "inculturation" of the Greek Patriarch Nestorius would have betrayed Divine Revelation. That is why he could no longer be bishop of Constantinople. He had certainly understood that God is transcendent. He had not understood to what extent He is near, close to us, capable of communicating Himself intimately from the interior to our humble humanity. God is less the Totally Other than the Totally Similar: the one who created us in His own image. He is not the Stranger, but the All in All. He is not the Incommunicable, but the Supreme Communication: transcendent and imminent in the highest degree. We understand nothing of God if we underrate either one of these two correlative qualities. That is why Nestorius could no longer be supreme pastor in the East. The Church rid itself of one of these two cultural deformations that from time to time, across the centuries, tempt highly intelligent theologians, as the apostle Paul had already deplored.

Let us not be tossed to and fro by every wind of doctrine devised by the wickedness of men, in craftiness, according to the wiles of error. (Ephesians: 4:14).

The stern measures taken at Ephesus were necessary for the faith. When Christ says, "I," it is not as a human person more or less united to the Son of God who speaks. It is the Son of God Himself Who speaks in this humanity assumed for our sakes. It is His eternal, "I as God," that speaks through the mouth of a man within human history.

But what does "Holy Mary, Mother of God" mean for Mary and what does it mean for us?

What Kind of Grace for Mary?

For Mary, it is at one and the same time both a unique gift and one that can be shared.

Shared, for in becoming Mother of God, she established a new relation, an intimate and familiar relation with God: a personal relation wonderfully immediate. And such a familial connection is not a personal privilege, quite the contrary. Mary was called to intimacy with the Son of God made man, not to monopolize it or to grasp it as a possessive mother, but to share it with all.

She was raised to be "Mother of God," not to be a goddess, ontologically equal to God (a totally absurd hypothesis), but, on the contrary, to give that God that feebleness, that littleness, that humility, that capacity to suffer and die for us, which He did not have in His divine nature. She gave Him the means to reveal, in this way, His love for and His nearness to us. She made Him man with us and for us. She gave Him that solidarity whereby He redeems and saves us. She made Him a member of the human family: our brother.

This role as Mother of God the Savior, which made Mary the pioneer and the first in the line of the redeemed, is none the less unique.

Alone, she gave birth to God made man.

Alone, she initiated the admirable exchange between man and God that establishes redemptive intimacy.

Alone, she gave God humanity, and thus God to man. Her human maternity thus forged a new link, one unimaginable, organic, familial between God and men.

Alone, this woman was able to bend over a child: her son, who was also her God; and this function of mother gives her a unique communion with God Himself.

Unique, for other men are sons of God in Jesus Christ, brothers of Christ, but she is His mother without losing her condition as daughter of the Father, for she remains a creature.

To this God, who through her became an embryo, then an infant (without of course, ceasing to be God, without lessening His divinity)—to Him she vowed all the love and care that a mother lavishes on her child. The personal tie, the fundamental link of every mother with her child, had in her case, a divine dimension.

Mother of Mankind

But Mary's mission does not end there. A logic of love inspired the plan of God, Who had chosen her and would lead her still further. Her mission as Mother of God engaged her to be mother of all. For God made man becomes, by His divine condition, the chief, the head, the unifier and regenerator of all humanity divided by sin. In becoming the human mother of the Son of God, in whom we are one, sole, living being for all eternity, Mary contracted a unique solidarity with all mankind. She was called to become mother of all.

This vocation was to be realized progressively in time, for maternity is not something achieved in a moment. It does not drop down from the sky. It develops on earth, in the course of time. One is not born a mother, one becomes such.

This is true likewise for the divine maternity. Mary became the Mother of the Son of God from the moment of His conception. But she had to become so with her whole being, throughout the period of gestation during which she formed Him, then during Christ's infancy, when she nourished Him and awakened Him to the world of men.

But after this divine maternity, she was to contract a new maternity, an adoptive one with respect to all mankind.

Adoptive mothers know well that one does not become a mother without great exertion of soul and even of body, a total transformation which has both its sorrows and its joys.

Following the admirable exchange wherein God became man in her to have us partake of His divinity, Mary contracts another exchange no less admirable, but sorrowful, both for her Son and for herself, one that occurs on Calvary, where His profound solidarity with mankind reaches a new stage.

The Son of God then takes upon Himself the weight of our sins and of human suffering, to give us His holiness in exchange. He was made sin for us, says St. Paul (*2 Corinthians* 5:21), to make us just by His death and resurrection and to have us partake of His eternal life. Salvific love at one and the same time effects both our pardon and our divinization.

This then was the exchange: **by that death, she lost**

the best of sons, the Son of God, and received us in exchange, us sinners:

> *Woman, behold your son, Jesus tells her. (John 19:26).*

This word of Christ on Calvary involves Mary in a sorrowful birth-giving for a new maternity called for by redemptive solidarity, and by the very love of Jesus Christ for us.

The adoption of all was not an empty word for her. To all the brothers and sisters of Christ, she has extended her unique love for the best of sons, and she has not been ungenerous with it.

"One and the Same"

Mothers of families, who adopt a child in difficulty, have a heart to love it with the same love that they have for their own children. The father and mother of a family of eight children who had adopted two abandoned children during a journey to the Third World told me, on the occasion of the birthday of one of them:

"This child and the others are for us, one and the same."

So too for Mary, the love she has for her son Jesus, whom she formed of her flesh, and her love for us, her other children, is one and the same.

This perfect generosity of adoptive love that God sometimes puts into the hearts of men, Mary has realized perfectly.

God the Father loves us, His adopted ones, with the same love with which He loves His eternal Son. His total love makes no difference between the unique Son of the divine nature and these men in distress, whom He loves through Jesus.

A difference in nature makes no difference in love, for

it is proper that it transcend differences and inequalities.

This is true of Mary's love. It is true of the love of the Father Who inspired her.

A little Sister, who died quite young at Bethlehem not long ago, understood this quite well. Serene in the midst of her sufferings, she nonetheless asked herself what she would do upon arriving in Heaven. And one day she found her answer: "I will say to the Father: I am your son Jesus Christ!"

She had grasped this profound identity, this identity of love within which God the Father envelops us. She would arrive, like Jacob clothed in the garments of his elder brother Esau, clothed with Jesus Christ, identified with Him.

At the same time, we understand what Mary's experience was: an overwhelming adventure in faith, just as in our life.

Not in ignorance, for faith is not ignorance. God does not leave us in ignorance as to where we are going. . . in the night. He tells us enough so that we can orient ourselves in this night. There the light of His mystery filters through, like the light from a star.

God addressed Mary in accord with her liberty. This is the first thing that is evident in the Gospel of the Annunication as we have seen.

She received this Good News that she would have a son, her own child, as every noble woman desires to have.

But at the same time she learns that this son would be the Son of God, whose name, "Jesus," signifies Savior. He would come to save and to gather humanity within Himself, to make of it one family. In the joyful mystery of the Incarnation, the Annunication called her to her vocation as mother of mankind.

But in order that this maternity be accomplished, she had to go through the sorrowful mystery of Calvary.

In the hour when Jesus gives birth to the Church by

His suffering and by His death, when this Church is born from His side opened with a lance, Mary, with all her motherly heart participates in this sorrowful birth-giving. She loses her own son to receive all others: men who are sinners, the perpetrators of that very death.

He confides this adoption to the person of the beloved disciple: the only one who dared come to Calvary, but in him all men are confided to her.

"Behold you son." (John 19:27).

Universal and Personal

Why do these words of Jesus speak only of one son? Why does he say, in regards to John the Evangelist, "Behold your son" and not, "All men are your sons"?

Pope John Paul II answered this difficulty in his encyclical *Redemptoris Mater.* Every maternity is something essentially personal, he says in substance; it is not a collective thing, for a mother loves each of her children personally. Thus to represent us all, Jesus chose the disciple whom He loved: the only one who had enough love to follow Him to the foot of the cross.

Progressively, God enlarged the heart of Mary as He enlarges the heart of every mother. He enlarged hers to a unique, universal, divine dimension so that she could be mother to each of us personally.

Mary became the Mother of God to become the mother of all; we must not forget that, when reciting this fundamental formula of the **Hail Mary,** which introduces and forms the foundation for the prayer of petition: **Mother of God.**

CHAPTER 8

Pray For Us

Why Intercession?

"Pray for us (poor) sinners." The last request of the **Hail Mary** is an appeal for Mary's intercession. When we meet someone close to God, someone radiant, "a saint," we spontaneously ask them to pray for us. Their prayer, as a friend of God, gives us confidence for the future. Mary is more holy than all those whom we know. Better than the best, she loves us more than anyone. She is the best intercessor after Jesus Christ: or better, **with** Jesus Christ, **in** Jesus Christ.

What good is intercession since God loves us and knows our needs? As Our Lord says in the Gospel:

"Your Father knows what you need before you ask him." (*Matthew* 6:33).

God knows, but He does not treat us like receptacles to be filled automatically, but as persons who communicate in a loving relationship. He invites us to ask.

"Ask and you shall receive." (*Matthew* 7:7).

"Ask and it shall be given to you; seek, and you shall find; knock and it shall be opened to you...What father among you, if his son asked for a fish, would hand him a snake? Or if he asked for an egg, hand him a scorpion?" (*Luke* 11:9-12).

"Whatever you ask for in my name, I will do."
(John 14:13).

"Ask whatever you will and it shall be done to you." (John 15:7,16; John 16:26).

"Not so!" you say. "Often, God does not grant what we ask."

And yet, if Christ insists on this point, it is because it is true.

There is need for us to ask as we should, for a father and mother whose child asks for something bad know how to refuse him. If he asks for a serpent or a scorpion that looks to him like a fine toy, his parents will refuse to give it.

Accordingly, our Heavenly Father and our Mother Mary do likewise. We must then learn how to discern, to desire what God wants to give us, and what Mary knows in him: what is best.

For God is not isolation and does not invite us to isolation. He is participation. He loves to have us participate with our whole soul in forming ourselves and our future. He loves to see us helping ourselves, and helping one another, asking things for one another.

The power of intercession is a current of love in which God loves to communicate. And at the summit of intercession, there is Mary with her Son Jesus Christ, our God. John the Evangelist has depicted her in this attitude of intercession, which she maintains ever since the Wedding of Cana (John 2).

Country weddings are a time of abundance, where people set out all that is needed to gratify their friends generously. Mary's keen and helpful eye saw that the wine skins were empty. She addresses Jesus whose human attention was further removed from these details.

"They have no wine," she says. Her request expresses a wish for the guests invited to the wedding, which will end calamitously, for it is humiliating to disappoint friends who have been invited to share family joy.

But Jesus puts her to the test. He responds enigmatically: *"Woman, what is that to me and to you? My hour is not yet come."*

The answer is a negative one.

The first part brushes the request aside. The underlying Hebrew expression—literally "What to me and to thee?"—is the one the demons use in asking him to keep away from them: *"What to me and to thee, Jesus of Nazareth, are you come to destroy us?"* (*Mark* 1:24).

The second part of the answer is a decisive objection: Jesus' hour, the hour of the cross, the hour of his death, from which the Resurrection will rise, *"is not yet come."*

Mary does not allow herself to be rebuffed. Jesus' reserve implants hope within her and perseverance in interceding. She rises above the test of this apparent refusal. She does not further press Jesus, who ends the dialogue.

She has confidence in him and addresses herself to the waiters, alerting them: *"Do whatever he tells you."* (*John* 2:5).

She knows very well that he is going to do something: "Ask and you shall receive."

And in accord with her request, he performs (he anticipates) his first sign: one that will establish the faith of his disciples: *"This, the first of his signs, Jesus did at Cana in Galilee. He manifested his glory and his disciples believed in him."* (*John* 2:12).

Let us not allow ourselves to be rebuffed; let us not allow ourselves to be discouraged when the Lord tries us. Let us persevere in confidence. Let us appeal to Mary's intercession, which has not changed since Cana. Let us listen to her constant invitation:

"Do whatever he tells you." (*John* 2:5).

CHAPTER 9

Sinners

We pray to the All Holy One, we who are sinners. Do we take cognizance of this?

Our age has lost the consciousness of sin. It would gladly remove this word from the **Hail Mary** as an unwelcome word. But the Church keeps it and must keep it. Furthermore, the French translation accentuates it with a piteous adjective: "poor" sinners.

We must first ask God for light on our sinfulness so that we do not pray as people unaware, without conviction. Let us ask God to discover our misery.

At most, our age accepts a culpability that is global, indistinct, and not responsible. "The sin of the world" wherein we exist, and of which everyone and no one is guilty, is a sinful environment, of which we are the unsuspecting and powerless victims and not the perpetrators.

God demands of us a more precise and more responsible consciousness. He loves us, He has given us everything, His life and His death. He gives Himself without reserve in the Eucharist. What a difference between this love and our response. Sin is essentially this lack of love and the lack of clarity that accompanies it, with so many consequences. Infractions, errors are the consequences, and we must be aware of this. The solution is to love more, for he who loves others, he who loves his neighbor has fulfilled the whole law. (*Romans* 13:8).

We must know where our sin lies: be it a serious or a slight fault. Sin is where there is responsibility. And we very often do not understand our responsibilities. Negligent ignorance is culpable in whatever situation. It must be guarded against.

When a person grows in holiness, he does not grow in complacency and admiration of himself. In the measure that we approach God, we at the same time gauge how far we are from His love and holiness. If we wish to leave sin, we must be aware of it, and the first grace to ask for is "light," for a fault perceived and regretted is already more than half pardoned and more than half cured.

The first condition for being cured of sin is clarity, then humility, for we do not like to see ourselves as we are, or to see where the trouble lies.

The second condition is hope. A hope greater than our misery, greater than our weakness, greater than the impossible: *"God is greater than our hearts,"* says the Apostle John (*1 John* 3:20).

Let us then open our heart to this double draft of air: humility and hope. Thus we will increase our chance of being heard when we ask Mary: Pray for us sinners.

The most tragic, the most radical evil is to be a sinner before God and not to be holy with our thrice holy Creator.

CHAPTER 10

Now

The **Hail Mary** situates the "pray for us sinners" in two time zones.

— the most proximate
— the most distant:
— "Now and at the hour of our death."

The Everyday

"Now": It is the everyday that is important. The Gospel invites us to live one day at a time: "Be not solicitous for tomorrow. Sufficient for the day is its own trouble." (*Matthew* 6:34). The everyday is banal, but banality is not mediocrity. It is in the everyday that the harvest grows. It is in the banality of the workshop of Nazareth that Jesus spent nine-tenths of His human life, without the least incident. The everyday has as its importance to form in us the stature and love that will be our eternity.

The everyday is not at all limited to our personal needs. It implies those of our family, our milieux. Each one must determine what these are and place them in the heart of Mary, our mother.

But there are also the needs of the Church and of the world. Let us not narrow down this vast horizon. The world has immense needs. It has abandoned itself to sin. Thus it is digging its own grave. Greed, violence and eroticism blaze heedlessly and contribute to this.

The present "now," at the approach of the third millennium, is a serious situation.

The Presence of Mary

This "now" also reminds us of Mary's presence. She is present as a mother who does not cease to think of us. There is never a "now" that escapes her, as she fully participates in God, the all in all.

Let us consider this maternal attention of Mary. Love is active. Mary's love acts for us depending on the current of love that moves reciprocally. Grace is not to be compared to a conduit for canalizing water. Communication is by way of interpersonal exchange. This presupposes, on one part, that we ask with a desire, confidence, receptivity.

Mary is constantly present to us. This is not a foolish idea. It is a truth of faith: Mary is the creature closest to God and by this title, the one closest to all others. She has the first place in the Mystical Body of Christ, which began in germ when the Son of God took form in her body, and when she was the first to give Him that adhesion in faith that establishes the Mystical Body of Christ. He gave her the function of mother and the means to fulfill it, beginning with the love He gives to mothers in the measure their marvelous task requires.

It would be well to give attention to this presence founded in faith. Over the centuries, many saints have been aware of it and have drawn fruit from it. Saint Ambrose already speaks of this presence.

Saint Germain of Constantinople (634-733) speaks of the experience in these words:

"You live completely with God. You have left the world without abandoning those who are in the world. Thrice blessed are those who delight in your visible presence (literally, who live with you) and those who know how to find you as mother of life! You live with us in spirit. The powerful protection wherewith you cover us is the sign of your presence among us. We all hear your voice, and our voices reach your ear. We all know you through your aid, and we recognize your powerful and ever present assistance." (*Homily on the Dormition,* pg. 98, 344-345).

And Saint John Damascene writes:

"Let us then make our memories a choice resting place for the Virgin Mary. . . Mary will often visit her faithful servants, bringing with her all things together with Christ her son, king and master of all, who lives in our hearts." (*Homily on the Assumption,* pg. 96, 752).

The grace of the presence of Mary was widespread during the seventeenth century, continuing with Grignon de Montfort. In the nineteenth century, Thérèse de Lixieux lived "completely hidden beneath the mantle of the Virgin Mary," during a particularly fruitful period of her life.

"The habitual presence of the Blessed Virgin is a gift, like the gift of the habitual presence of God, quite rare it is true, accessible nevertheless to one who is very faithful," said William Joseph Chaminade (*The Spirit of our Foundation,* v. 1, p. 174).

It is not an emotional presence, but one lived in faith, in obscurity.

It is not the presence of God, which is a creative presence. God alone causes us to exist. He alone gives us existence at each moment to such an extent, that if he ceased to think of us, we would cease to exist—the way our dreams vanish when we awake. At each instant, Christ, God Savior, directly communicates His divine life, His life of love.

Mary does not accede to this divine and transcendent role. Her presence is not of the metaphysical order, but of the moral order. It is a presence of love and action, with God, in God and by God: a maternal presence which is exercised with a special delicacy.

Normally this presence has both its strong and weak moments. The strong moments are analogous to those which it had in the life of Jesus. Mary is first of all the Virgin of beginnings. She was the one chiefly involved at the birth of Jesus and in His infancy. She obtains the first miracle of Jesus at Cana of Galilee (*John* 2:1-12). She was present at the birth of the Church at Pentecost (*Acts* 1:14; 2:1-12). It is fitting that we too offer her the beginnings of our projects and of our actions.

She is also the Virgin of transitions. It is through her that the way was made from the Old to the New Testament, by the coming of Christ. Her presence at Calvary and then with the Apostles until Pentecost attends the way from Christ to the Church; and her Assumption anticipates that of the Church at the Parousia. Thus, we must confide to her the transitions of our lives, the difficult and decisive moments.

She is especially the Virgin of sorrowful transitions. She is the Virgin of the "Stabat," at the foot of the cross, where she was given to us as mother. In our trials and at the hour of our death, her function is to bring peace and hope. Let us learn how to discover this presence of Mary in the communion of saints. This is the first and most loving presence after that of God, in the action of the Holy Spirit, within whom she lives and acts.

CHAPTER 11

And at the Hour of Our Death

The Inescapable

"And at the hour of our death." These are the last words of the **Hail Mary.** They invite us to think about the last moment of our life—disquieting and inescapable.

Death is our most certain rendezvous. Our civilizations for a long time have tried to disguise it or cause it to be forgotten.

Death, indescribable, is covered over by ostentatious burial places. It is caricatured in a death's head, or in a skeleton made to look somewhat strong so it can wield a scythe. These representations try to exorcise our anxiety before the unknown, the void, the final engulfment; for we do not see death and what follows after, any more than we see the other side of our mirrors.

What is death?

Death remains an enigma for science. Doctors have tried to define it without arriving at an adequate solution.

1. At first the criterion was the stopping of the heart. But the heart can start up again. . .and we must avoid burying a living person whose heart would start up inside a coffin or in the depths of a grave. My grandmother feared this and had asked my brother, a doctor, to burn her little

finger before placing her on a bier. This he did conscientiously. The finger began to burn like the wick of a candle.

2. More recently it has been said that a flat encephalogram denotes all cessation of cerebral activity. But a flat encephalogram can at times start up again.

3. In short, only the corruption of the body establishes death with certainty.

One day a priest asked a suicidal drug addict who persisted in destroying herself: "But why?"

And she answered with some heat: "Don't you understand that everyone must die? Anything that will free us from this anguish is good."

Our Death

The **Hail Mary** has the courage to name "death," and after naming it, to appropriate it: OUR death.

We use the first person plural and not the first person singular: not my death but our death. It is fitting to assume the common lot, in solidarity with our parents, our friends, above all with Christ who died for us. We form an immense cortege. But at its head, there is the risen Christ, and not the death's head with its sickle. His death and resurrection are given to us (inserted into us) by communion.

Another Birth

Death is no longer that source of bewilderment, that ghastliness, that fathomless abyss if we look at it in faith from Mary's perspective and that of Christ; for they have experienced it without giving way in a paroxysm of distress. They teach us to look upon it in peace and with love, from God's point of view.

According to this second view, death is no longer desolation, an empty and final end. It is a beginning, hope, promise. It is a new birth.

This is what a child about to be born experiences in his elementary consciousness, when he feels the shocks that expel him from the warm, dark milieu where he grew, out into the unknown that he is ignorant of. What seizes him then can only be anguish: for birth is something violent just as death is.

And for all that, this difficult passage, this exile outside the maternal womb, a climate-controlled milieu, where the infant had grown, where he heard the lulling of a familiar voice, is the passport towards autonomy and liberty. It is also the discovery of his mother, no longer as an anonymous milieu, evidence of an unknown beyond, but as someone face to face, a visage, a smile, a communication from person to person. It is the discovery of light.

Such also is death: a way towards the light, if we have known how to welcome the light.

Life after Life

Some people have had the fleeting experience of being in the beyond. In the course of accidents, that have for a time taken them from their bodies, they have seen the inert corpse which they have left, and caught a glimpse of a road of light leading towards an inexpressible Being of Light.

These experiences that have impressed our era, which has become such a stranger respecting the beyond, are only a foretaste. They have been able to make perceptible only the threshold of Heaven. Our blasé society, which views the beyond only as nothingness, has become excited about this sign familiar to our ancestors. For the first time it has become the object of coherent and sustained study.

These experiences are fascinating, but ambiguous. Those who return were certainly not completely dead. They have experienced a certain autonomy of soul, its transcendence with respect to the body, its immortality. But this was only an anteroom of life.

Dr. Moody and his successors, who have rendered service in exploring these frontier experiences (more frequent than one might suppose), have recently taken a Gallop poll. The threshold speaks to us. It challenges the vision that a materialist culture has so largely imposed on us.

These fugitive and debatable signs are not the basis for our assurance in respecting the beyond that is light. It is rather the word of God. It is the infinite light of God. To the degree that we have opened our heart to Him, to the degree that we live with Him, that with Him we bear fruit, and that in this way our life has found His light beyond the darkness of sin, we discover the certitude that God Himself gives concerning the future and the fervor to live in His service during the short time that we have to live here below. Such was the certitude of Thérèse of Lisieux. Sunk in the darkness of suffering and dereliction, she said on her death bed: "I am entering into life."

To Desire Death?

After the·first apparition of the Blessed Virgin at Medjugorje, little Jakov, aged ten, said spontaneously: "Ah, now, I shall no longer have any fear of dying!"

He was speaking like Bernadette, who was asked about the Blessed Virgin's beauty: "So beautiful that one would have been willing to die to see her again."

And yet the beauty of Mary is only a reflection of the light of God. It is then not unnatural to speak to Mary about our death. She knows the dark side of death, such as was that of Christ beneath the weight of our sins: an agonizing death, humiliating, the death of one condemned, nailed to a cross, torn, transpierced, a concentration of all horrors, disgrace and all sorrows. But she also knows its victory, its results and the coming forth of light.

She is our mother. She knows our anxieties and the secret of calming them. Mothers have secrets for calming distress. The best of mothers has received all of God's secrets for this purpose.

We see only the dark and vertiginous side of death, the black side: coffin, burial, absence, expulsion from a world which continues frenetically and which will gradually forget us.

Mary is well aware of what grips us at the hour of death, such as we perceive it from our viewpoint. But she also knows where we are going: to the other side of the mirror, God's side, the side where there is love without shadow, the side of light and life.

With everything else, let us entrust to her our death.

CHAPTER 12

Amen

The final "Amen" (which used to be translated by the expression "thus may it be"), signifies more than that pious wish. This Hebrew word is an adhesion to the unshakable constancy of God beyond our frailties, our inconstancy.

This word which the Church teaches us to say at the end of our prayers, Jesus repeated at the beginning of his most solemn discourses in order to attest to the divine and unimpeachable truth.

"Amen, amen, I say to you," as we find in *John* 1:52 and twenty times in all throughout this Gospel and often in the other Gospels. His "Amen" was intended to replace the initial phrase used by the prophets: *Thus says the Lord.* Jesus, who speaks on his own with the authority of God, expresses a more immediate, a more incontrovertible certainty. By this word he attests to two things: His word is truth—He himself is the truth.

Faith, in Hebrew *emunah,* is formed from this root *aman.* For in the Bible, according to revelation, faith is not a foolhardy wager, it is the principal certitude that comes from God. The word signifies firmness, stability, the certitude of faith, however it may appear to us. We do not always experience its benefit, for our human psychology is fragile and tormented. Faith is an objective certitude, founded on the transcendence of God who speaks. His word is truth, and His interior light enables us to adhere firmly to this truth. It demands this confidence from us (such as was the confidence of Orpheus who would be able to free Eurydice from the underworld on condition that he not look at her). It is an adhesion to the truth of God, to the certitude that He gives us of things unseen and mysterious.

While adhering to God in faith, we may have the impression that it is all a wager, a dream. Here below, God ordinarily teaches us that we have reason to believe. He has us grasp this by signs that His light illumines, according to the measure of our fidelity, however severe certain trails may be.

That is why it is fitting to conclude every prayer with this "Amen." We say yes without hesitation, without afterthought, to the truth of the hidden God, yes to his proposals of love, to his teachings: a firm yes, founded on the unshakable. May our adhering love respond without vacillating to the firmness of His interior testimony, and His love.

Such is the example of Mary's faith: a decisive "Amen" given to the Word of God, irrevocably involved in the realization of the redemptive incarnation.

A MARVELOUS RICHNESS THAT SURPASSES US

The richness of Christian prayer can be overwhelming when a person examines it in detail and studies it deeply.

"If I must think of all that when reciting the **Hail Mary,** it's better to leave it alone," one is tempted to say.

Certainly, you cannot think of everything when reciting this prayer, just as one does not spell out the thousand and one secrets of a beautiful countryside that one admires, and that a guide book would list. But an explanation is not at all useless, especially when it clarifies and goes deeply into the matter. It enables us to realize the weight of gold with which the words are filled; all the weight of the mystery of the Incarnation, and of its revelation to Mary at the time of the Annunciation; all the weight of the Old Testament which was fulfilled there. It embodies all the weight of the meditation of Mary, who kept these words and events in her heart (*Luke* 2:19, 51), a biblical meditation that led up to the Gospel put together by Luke; all the weight of Christian generations, who have formed and recited this prayer and repeat it uninterruptedly millions of times a day, trillions of times since it was established in the Church.

If these words surpass us, they remain simple and have nothing overwhelming in them. It is good to understand them according to their true measure.

So too our body is formed from billions of cells; the brain, the instrument of our intelligence, is composed of 30 billion neurons, so numerous that each day we lose some thousands of them without harm. We cannot comprehend this organic richness when we think. It is good to understand what has been given to us, spoiled children, in a world created for us, as the Bible states (*Genesis* 1), but also spoiled children of salvation who have driven Christ even to death.

After all that, in the daily round of our little lives and our feeble psychologies as rational animals, we can only stammer like children in giving thanks to God, Creator and Savior, for all that He gives us, for all that He is preparing for us to perceive in Him one day in full light.

In all humility let us poor sinners learn how to stammer with the poor the **Hail Mary,** the **Our Father,** which the Lord himself has taught us, and the **Glory be** to the praise of His glory.

PRAYERS BASED ON THE HAIL MARY

The **Hail Mary** is a familiar prayer, forming a part of many others in which the Virgin Mary has her place and especially important in two of them, recommended constantly by the Church, and by the last few Popes.

The Rosary

The Rosary is so called because its initiator, Alain de la Roche, saw in it a triple crown of roses offered to Mary. It is a poetic name.

The Rosary is composed of one hundred fifty **Hail Marys** to accord with the one hundred and fifty psalms that it is meant to replace.

It is then a popular prayer, the breviary of the poor, the illiterate of that time, who had only their memory with which to pray.

The Rosary links together three segments of five decades of **Hail Marys** preceded by the **Creed** (an expression of faith), followed by an **Our Father** and three **Hail Marys** in honor of the three Persons of the Holy Trinity.

Each decade begins with the **Our Father** and ends by glorifying the Trinity, the beginning and the end of all things:

> Glory to the Father and to the Son and to the Holy Spirit. As it was in the beginning, is now and ever shall be world without end.

The Rosary is certainly not meant to be a quantitative performance. The mechanical movement of the lips, which cannot be attentive to each word (save during a contemplative recitation), serves as a base for meditating on the fifteen mysteries of the Rosary: Joyous, Sorrowful and Glorious.

These mysteries are a road through the entire Gospel: from the Annunciation to Pentecost, prolonged by an eschatological contemplation of the glory and the coronation of Our Lady, who goes before the Church.

All the mysteries then except the last two are biblical.

— The joyful mysteries: Annunciation, Visitation, Christmas, the Presentation and the Finding in the Temple.
— Sorrowful mysteries: The Agony in the Garden, the Scourging, the Crowning with Thorns, the Carrying of the Cross and the Crucifixion.
— Glorious mysteries: the Ressurection, the Ascension, Pentecost, the Assumption and Mary's Coronation.

What we have then is a Gospel meditation and not a particularist devotion. This devotion is so biblical, so evangelical, that Pastor Neville Ward, in his Methodist parish, introduced the Rosary shortly before 1970, with such success that he thereupon wrote a book, today translated into several languages (J. N. Ward, *Five for Sorrow,*

Ten for Joy, published in London in 1971 and in Turin, Italy, in 1973).

The Rosary was formed slowly from various forms of prayer, inaugurated during the twelfth and thirteenth centuries with the **Hail Mary** as a base. But it was the Dominican, Alain de la Roche, who gave it its final form at Douai in 1470, under the name Mary's Psalter. Others before him had adopted the number of one hundred fifty **Hail Marys,** according to the number of one hundred fifty psalms. His contribution was to reduce the number of mysteries to fifteen. And it was less a question of a formula for prayer, than of a communitarian movement: his confrères recited the rosary with a faith that moved mountains. There resulted many graces: union with God, service to God, cures, conversions, protection in danger.

The Dominicans have brought about a rebirth of the community movement, with Rosary circles, flourishing during the last few years despite the concurrence of many other prayer groups, whether charismatic or inspired by Medjugorje.

The Angelus

The *Angelus* is the recitation of the three **Hail Marys,** three times a day to celebrate the coming of Christ, at the Annunciation.

Each **Hail Mary** is preceded by a biblical antiphon:

> *"The angel of the Lord declared unto Mary and she conceived of the Holy Spirit." (Luke* 1:28, 35).

> *"Behold the handmaid of the Lord, let it be done to me according to your word." (Luke* 1:38).

> *"And the Word became flesh and dwelt among us." (John* 1:14).

These antiphons make quite explicit the setting and the meaning of the **Hail Mary,** just as we have explained in this book. The *Angelus* ends with the collect for the Feast of the Annunciation:

> Pour forth, we beseech You, O Lord, Your grace into our hearts; that, as we have known the Incarnation of Christ Your Son by the message of an Angel, so by His Passion and Cross we may be brought to the glory of His Resurrection. Through the same Christ our Lord. Amen.

The *Angelus* began in certain places during the eleventh century: but it was said only in the evening. Pope Gregory IX (d. 1241) ordered church bells to be rung to promote prayer for the Crusades. In 1269 Saint Bonaventure recommended the Franciscan custom of saying three **Hail Marys** when the evening bell sounded. John XXII granted an indulgence for this practice in 1318.

The morning *Angelus* appears to derive from the first sound of the bell for the hour of Prime in monasteries.

The *Angelus* at midday seems to have appeared to commemorate the Passion, at first only on Friday (according to the Synod of Prague in 1386). It was extended to the entire week by Calixtus III in 1456 at the time of the war with the Turks.

It was in the seventeenth century that the *Angelus* was made uniform and popularized in the form used today: three times a day, at morning, noon and evening. This mystery commemorates the beginning of salvation in Jesus Christ and Mary's unique role in this mystery.

OTHER PRAYERS

The Memorare

This prayer, attributed to Saint Bernard, is found only at the beginning of the fifteenth century, but it fixes a tradition that is doubtless much more ancient. This prayer was known by everyone and aroused great fervor. The most celebrated episode is the conversion of Alphonse Ratisbonne. On January 17, 1842, this young banker, a stranger to Christianity and a hostile one, was challenged to recite this prayer. Three days later, on January 20, he sees the Blessed Virgin as she appears on the Miraculous Medal. His life was changed by it. Here is the prayer:

> Remember, O most gracious Virgin Mary, that never was it known, that any one who fled to your protection, implored your help or sought your intercession, was left unaided. Inspired with this confidence, I fly unto you, O Virgin of virgins and Mother, to you do I come, before you I stand, sinful and sorrowful; O Mother of the Word Incarnate, despise not my petitions, but in your mercy hear and answer me. Amen.

My Queen, My Mother

A prayer of consecration through Mary, very popular in Christian families since the seventeenth century.

> My Queen! my Mother! I give thee all myself, and, to show my devotion to you, I consecrate to you my eyes, my ears, my mouth, my heart, my entire self. Wherefore, O loving Mother, as I am your own, keep me, defend me, as your property and possession.

PRAYING WITH MARY

Prayers addressed to Mary are not the only form, nor the highest form of prayer that unites us to her and draws down her intercession.

In the Church's most important prayers: the Canon of the Mass and in the orations, Mary appears as a motif for prayer. Such is her place in the *Angelus* collect, which we have just read. Similarly, all the canons and anaphoras of the present Mass mention her presence in the communion of saints: "In union with the whole Church, we venerate in the first place, the glorious Virgin Mary, Mother of God" as we find in a very ancient Eastern anaphora of the fourth century, source of the Mass called that of Saint Pius V.

Praying with Mary is also what the seers of Medjugorje do at her invitation. During each apparition she interrupts their colloquy with her by beginning the **Our Father.** They join in, with perfect synchronization and also recite with her the **Glory be to the Father.** For the seers, this is the high point of the apparition.

Faith Publishing Company

Faith Publishing Company is dedicated to the publishing and distribution of materials that reflect the teachings of the Catholic Church. For additional information on titles of books available, please write to THE RIEHLE FOUNDATION, distributor of Faith Publishing books.

Other titles available by Fr. René Laurentin include:

AN APPEAL FROM MARY IN ARGENTINA
The incredible story of the apparitions currently taking place in San Nicolás, Argentina. 160 pages.   **$6.00**

THE MESSAGES OF OUR LADY AT SAN NICOLÁS
The chronological listing of 1,800 messages received by the seer in San Nicolás. 420 pages.   **$7.00**

WHY PRAYER? AND HOW TO PRAY
A fresh, and simple look at the theology of prayer. A "why" and "how to" book. 96 pages.   **$4.00**

MESSAGES AND TEACHINGS OF OUR LADY
The chronological listing of the messages from Medjugorje with an in-depth analysis of how they tie in with Scripture and Catholic Doctrine. 325 pages.   **$7.00**

Write: THE RIEHLE FOUNDATION
        P.O. Box 7
        Milford, OH 45150